Guidebook To Your Heart

Mimi Novic

Aspiring Hope
Publishing

Copyright © Mimi Novic 2024

All rights reserved. No part of this publication may be reproduced, stored in a retrieval system, or transmitted in any form or by any means, electronic, mechanical, photocopy, recording or otherwise, without prior written permission of the copyright owner.
Nor can it be circulated in any form of binding or cover other than that in which it is published and without similar condition including this condition being imposed on a subsequent purchaser.

British Library Cataloguing Publication Data.

A Catalogue record for this book is available from the British Library.

ISBN 978-1-9999120-0-0

Published by Aspiring Hope Publishing

About The Author

Mimi Novic is one of today's bestselling inspirational authors and is ranked amongst the top names in inspirational, motivational and spiritual books in the world. Her writings and quotes are considered some of the most popular in modern times and are used by some of today's most well known and influential figures.

She is internationally known as one of the most respected and highly regarded motivational and self awareness teachers in the fields of self-development and spiritual growth. Her expertise has made her amongst the most popular and highly demanded well being experts of today.

Working as a psychotherapist, complementary medical practitioner, self development teacher, voiceover artist, author and motivational speaker, Mimi has collaborated with some of the most well-known and knowledgeable therapists, composers, musicians, coaches, healers and professionals in their field and bringing together powerful teams that work in synchronicity to bring the best possible life enhancing experiences.

She teaches and runs workshops and seminars in a wide array of therapies, complementary medicine and self-awareness, working around the world in clinics, retreats and on a one to one basis.

For more information about Mimi Novic please visit::
www.miminovic.co.uk

Dedication

In the Name of God the Most Beneficent the Most Merciful.

Everything about you reminded me of Love.
I'm wandering like the wind, Until we are united again.

Introduction

Life is a wonderful journey of discovery and adventure with many roads to travel to achieve inner peace and happiness.

If we pause and stand still for a moment to enjoy the amazing world that we are part of we realise that everything is unfolding as it should and that there are lessons in life that teach us to be more fulfilled and to take every chance that makes us feel alive.

We all have days that we feel different feelings depending on the circumstances that we find ourselves in and these inspiring, joyful and thought provoking messages will remind you that your heart is your compass in every situation, that leads to light and love.

We are all unique and our presence is a gift to those we meet along the way.

When we believe in ourselves we find the real treasure...Our heart.

Enjoy Life. Live Life. Love Life.

Contents

Chapter 1	You Are Unique
Chapter 2	Loneliness
Chapter 3	Fear
Chapter 4	Sadness
Chapter 5	Anger
Chapter 6	Uncertainty
Chapter 7	Guidance
Chapter 8	Faith
Chapter 9	Hope
Chapter 10	Happiness
Chapter 11	Aspiration
Chapter 12	Your Power
Chapter 13	Encouragement
Chapter 14	Embrace Your Heart
Chapter 15	Unlocking Love

CHAPTER 1
You Are Unique

It starts from within us.
Yet everyone looks outside of themselves.
Everything you need is within you.

Always be different.
Always be you.

The world needs you.
There is only one of you
amongst all the stars and planets
that can do what you do.

When you are brave enough to stand up for who you are and be yourself,
Life becomes so much easier.

Your path can only ever be for you.
Start walking towards your destiny.

CHAPTER 2
Loneliness

To see the beautiful and mystical
in the other worlds,
One first must see the beauty of
one's own soul.

Your path becomes light,
When you trust your inner being.

Tears are the same in every language.
Everyone is fighting a battle we know nothing about.
Be patient with yourself and those you meet.

Do everything like it's the first time and you will always enjoy the joy of that moment.

What gives the desert its
beautiful freedom?
It is that it accepts its state of
total solitude and therefore
knows the secrets of itself.

CHAPTER 3
Fear

You are not alone.
You are the stardust of the entire universe.

People are so afraid to lose, they don't even try to win.
Don't be defeated before you even begin.

Every positive change in your life,
Begins with the first step.

We learn and grow through
overcoming
our shadows and our fears.

In the end we will only ever regret the chances we never took.
Take the chance.

CHAPTER 4

Sadness

There are no mistakes, only lessons.
Set yourself free.
Believe in the beauty of your life.

We must never forget,
We all have a purpose in this life.

If it doesn't bring you peace,
Then it's not for you.

While there is breath there is hope.
Keep travelling every road and taking every journey until you meet yourself.

Our days are full of divine
meetings with each other.
We must be open at all times so
we do not miss them.

CHAPTER 5

Anger

Make a decision to always choose peace whatever situation you find yourself in.

Don't throw away your days on what doesn't make you happy. Do everything in your power to cherish moments that bring you happiness and love.

Be kind to yourself.
Nothing is worth losing your peace.

Change your perspective on every situation you come across and you will see the reality of everything.

Never stay anywhere where you are not appreciated, nor understood.
Celebrate your self worth and move on.

CHAPTER 6

Uncertainty

When we begin to trust ourselves we begin to live our best life.

You are never in the wrong place.
Sometimes you are in the right place looking at things in the wrong way.

It's the journey that matters,
Sometimes even more than the
destination.

Every heart has a wish.
Let the angels hear your song
and take it to God's door.

People may not understand your words,
But they will always feel your soul.

CHAPTER 7
Guidance

Sometimes we only know where we are going,
When we arrive.

We cannot choose how many
moments our life has,
But we can choose how much
life our moments have.

Every day fall in love with being alive.

Nothing in life is ever a
coincidence,
Trust God's timing.

The only way to really value our
time on earth,
Is to remember that everything
is momentary.

CHAPTER 8
Faith

The most valuable treasures we have are not visible to the outside world.

We look a lifetime for answers to help us understand our existence,
But we forget that our life is the answer.

Everything you need is here right now.
Don't wait for the moment.
You are the moment.

You have the power within you
to rise above whatever is seeking
to bring you down.

Sometimes we have to take a leap of faith to be given the opportunity to discover our wings.

CHAPTER 9

Hope

Those that pass through our life often show us something new about ourselves.

Sometimes we choose the road we follow.
Sometimes the road chooses us.

Your life is the proof that you have a purpose.
You are the treasure that you are searching for.

When we make friends with ourselves,
The bridge between ourselves and others carries us closer to one another.

We were each presented with
the book of our life before we
came to earth.
When we look closely we can be
inspired by what was promised
to our soul.

CHAPTER 10
Happiness

Search for the beauty of this world,
There is so much to see, feel and enjoy.

Everything we can touch with
our hands disappears into the
fragments of time.
What we touch with our heart
lasts eternally.

The power is within you.
Do everything with love,
Success will always follow.

Within the desert of this lonely world your soul is the oasis of love.

Be gentle with yourself,
Your presence here is a journey
of discovery.

CHAPTER 11

Aspiration

The greatest opportunities are always somewhere where you least expect them to be.

Do what makes you feel alive every day.
Your heart always wants to be where it is free to fly.

Have courage to ride on the wings of destiny and let them be your guide.

We all have a divine spark that guides us,
We just need to set it alight.

You are an ambassador of love.
Let your whole being illuminate
the world with its presence.

CHAPTER 12
Your Power

You are priceless.
Your worth is beyond measure.
Accept yourself and flourish.

Unless we push our own limits
we will never know what amazing
things we can achieve.

Just as the moon changes, yet
remains the same,
We can also change to become
our true selves.

We are all born with a talent that
is a gift to the world.
We just have to discover it.

Trust God endlessly.
Believe in yourself without limits.
Endure every obstacles with patience.
Hope for the best in every single moment.

CHAPTER 13

Encouragement

True beauty shines from your heart,
Reflecting your light from within.

In this moment we are alive and this moment is all that matters.

Courage comes quietly.
Faith roars silently.
Love comes unexpectedly.

Nothing is a waste of time if you use the experience wisely.

Everything that we touch with our soul becomes a part of our essence.

CHAPTER 14

Embrace Your Heart

Discover who you are and enjoy the freedom it brings.

Trust the feeling inside and you will always find the way.

Don't be afraid to live,
You are here to be exhilarated
and celebrated.

The day is full of beautiful things waiting to happen. Embrace each one with open arms.

There are times when we don't
need to say anything.
We just need to feel everything.

CHAPTER 15

Unlocking Love

Life is too short.
Be with someone who takes
your breath away.
Anything else isn't worth a
second of your time.

The only real thing in our life that lasts forever is love.

Love is a powerful key.
Use it to unlock all the doors
along your destiny.

When the heart opens its doors to love,
The whole universe awakens to welcome it.

Be with those that give your wings the wind of hope and accept your uniqueness.